AuthorHouse™
1663 Liberty Drive
Bloomington, IN 47403
www.authorhouse.com
Phone: 1 (800) 839-8640

Published by AuthorHouse 06/05/2015

ISBN: 978-1-5049-0470-4 (sc)
978-1-5049-0471-1 (e)

Library of Congress Control Number: 2015905554

Print information available on the last page.

authorHOUSE®

FOR YOU

By

Ana J. García

DEDICATION

I dedicate this book of poems to you, the reader. The poems are my experiences and memories from my childhood, my love life and travels to other countries. Each day I have lived I have lived to the fullest since I do not know the day of my transition.

Nature has been my teacher. A butterfly and a rose live a short and perfect life. The sunrises are the promises of a brand new day and the sunsets the end of all the problems of each passing day.

Nature is filled with multicolor flowers that decorate our gardens and can heal or kill us. In nature we find soothing sounds, and terrain that resemble oriental tapestry or extraterrestrial messages.

It is my wish you find a constant joy in your sunrises and sunsets, and in every tree, flower and bird song.

Let every breath you take be like the first breath you took when you came into the world. ***Just be in the moment.***

ACKNOWLEDGMENTS

I would like to express my gratitude to:

Abba, my heavenly Father, who created me and has been with me every step of the way.

Carlos and Nélida, my parents. I came through them and they cared for me until Abba called them home.

Bishop E. Bernard Jordan, who made me angry enough to tear off the façade and see myself as God's creation in all my potentiality.

Nyugen Smith, for his patience in teaching me Photoshop and critiquing my art work.

Therefore I say unto you, Take no thought for your life, what ye shall eat, or what ye shall drink; nor yet for your body, what ye shall put on. Is not the life more than meat, and the body than raiment?

Behold the fowls of the air: for they sow not, neither do they reap, nor gather into barns; yet your heavenly Father feedeth them. Are you not much better than they?[1]

Matthews 6:25-26

---

[1] *Good News Bible with Deuterocanocicals/Apocrypha.* Matthew 6:25-26. (New York: American Bible Society, 1976)

CONTENTS

NATURE

SPIRIT, SOUL AND BODY

LOVE, A MASTERPIECE AT WORK

EACH DAY A CANVAS

NATURE

A MORNING WITH THE MASTERS

1/21/1985

I wake up and as I move I notice
that even the air I breath is different.

The sky is of a lead blue,
and
the city is like a painting of the masters.

I see Van Gogh
in the lines drawn by the sidewalks;
in the old buildings.

I see Monet
in the different hues of pink and blue;
in the dove gray combined with shades of browns and oranges.

In my delirium of happiness
all melts into Dali's surrealistic painting
of timeless memories.

The breeze engulfs me
whispering merry tunes of love.

My body throbs to the rhythm of the beauty before me.

APHRODISIAC COLORS
11/1/85

Visual and acoustic aphrodisiacs
are
the marvelous hues
of green, yellow,
orange and brown
that
meander like a multitude of serpentines in a prairie.

The green and the yellow
make me feel revitalized
with
the new life that is inside of me.

The orange and brown
transport me to a quiet and warm place
where we become one
to leave behind the duality
and
for a moment
become
ecstasy,
perfection,
and love in the afternoon.

The wind shakes the leaves
and
seeing them fall
remind me of the
pastoral,
angelic,
purified,
symphony
forever immortal.

THE DOG, FAITHFUL FRIEND
7/2010

It's noon.
Everyone rests.
I seat at the marina.
It's cool and it is sunny.
The sea reflects its rays.
All is peace around me.

Total contrast
to the national and international
man's barbarity
which I read
on today's
newspaper.

I am lucky
to hear only
the sound of the boats and its bells
being swayed by the sea.

My dog, faithful friend, is by my side.
He keeps me company.
He protects me.
No one can come near me.

His presence reminds me
that now,
today,
I am happy.

MY FRIEND, THE RAIN
8/15/85

The leaves of the tree changes its emerald color to a lighter green
letting us know the rain is near.

Oh! Rain!

You are a faithful friend in afternoons of love.

You are the veil that hides us,
a magical concert played only for us.

You are the reminder of the many times that
I
like
you
aphrodisiacally
bathed his pearly soft skin.
I would slide down
slowly, gently
reaching the most hidden places
of his skin where
I wallowed
and
lost myself
in the excitement.

Oh! Rain!
You remind me of so many things….!

EMERALD GREEN PRAIRIES

Emerald green prairies…
Huts of henequen…
wild flower, national butterfly…
sprinkling stream, small broom that gently sweeps the rocks
and hum various musical themes...

Colts stirred up; friends of their masters;
partners at work;
confidants in nights of debauchery and drunkenness
faithful in danger.

I am riding my white horse that snorts.
By me my dog barks.
Snorts and barking
an exchange of friendship.
What joy! Friends, my partners!

BROOK AND ROCKS
2/2011

Brook from the high mountain range
you come branching off
and
blessing fauna and flora.

I hear you as I approach
the forest that cool and serene
fills me with joy and fantasy.

I arrive.
The light of the sun reflects
on your pure water.
PRANA.
Life's flow.

The rocks
of various colors and forms
are
precious gems.
Legacy that we leave
for
future generations.

3/30/85

Night bird, freely you fly.
White plumage, tiger's eyes.
Sharp talon, life's support.

STREAMLET FLOWING
7/2011

Gentle streamlet
by your waterfall I cool off.

To think that in a split second
like a monster
you would devour me.

WINTRY, WINDY NIGHT
3/9/87

Wintry, windy night
skeletal tree
with promise of
spring budding.

SYMPHONY OF THE STARS
12/22/86

Nomadic equestrian that in the lonely night

find rest

resting in a turquoise prairie.

You play your guitar and sing the beauty of your soul.

The honey mesquite nearby and the stars listen to you.

The wind goes silent and its soft breeze refreshes you.

The faithful dog watches

and you sleep lulled

by

the dazzling symphony astral

on

the velvety stage of the universe.

THE RIVER AND THE EBB TIDE

River waters
that from a spring births.

River waters
that joins the sea.

Diurnal waters that at night rise
to the command
of mother moon.

Rise, rise,
divine splendor.

Rise, rise,
purity and chastity.

NAVY BLUE

[Inspiration – *El Concierto de Aranjuez*]

Sky, you are close to me.
Why can't you see the sadness that paralyzes me?

Sky, you are a fountain of joy and a faithful companion.
Why don't you bring me someone
that shares all with me as I do with you?

Sky, brother, if you are grey,
I sing to make you happy.
Today, it is I who is dressed in gray,
And I need your song.

Hurry!
Find my lover
so you shine with the light of my joy;
of eternal love in all its splendor.

GEISHA OF THE NIGHT

3/16/1987

Geisha of the night
nocturnal madam
seductive lover
only you shine in your dark room

Flirtatiously you appear
from behind the illuminated skyscrapers
embedded in jade, pearls, and rubies
intensifying the desire of the ones who admire you.

You appear and your brilliancy bewitches.

What arrogance! What elegance!

MY DIAMOND

I am a country woman.
I diligently cultivate the land.
What is this?
What an interesting rock!

I will take it home
and
I will clean it.
I will polish it slowly
so it shines
like no other.

THE SKY, MY FRIEND?

Faithful friend and partner
you wear blue.
Your strength refreshes and energizes me.

I am not your friend.
You become sad!
You cry profusely
and I take advantage.
I live my best moments.

GREEN GRASS, RUNNING FREE....

In the recess of my mind
I can only see the beautiful green grass
spread out, wild, open to the sky.

I also lay on it with my friend and partner
in perfect harmony.
The space is so vast that we forget
all the reckless, inhibiting morals
created by a confused mind
who never knew the purity
of loving with all its might
in unison with the rhythm of nature
in a
Bacchanal Feast.

I DREAM
3/30/85

I dream that I am dreaming
I am whatever others want me to be.

I dream that I am wandering in the darkness
because I only exist in someone else's world.

Others don't even know why they exist.

I exist and don't know why.

I approach a garden
and
in the reflection of a lilac chrysanthemum
I see my reflection
and
I exist
at the moment.

I recognize myself
even if it is just
by looking at
my eyes, my mouth and my hair.

I am, because with my eyes
I see the world that is part of my being.
Earth, wind and fire,
all the elements that are part of my body.

My mouth expresses
the beauty of life,
exhorts others to live each day to the fullest,
and spreads my joy.

I walk
and
my hair plays
with the breeze,
flirts with it,
and dances to its uncontrollable rhythm.

I look,
I fear
and
leave
others to dream,
to create
their own reality.

THE SACRED FOUNTAIN
7/2011

My cabin is in a green and cool forest.
My dinner is the fruit of the earth.
My fireplace warms me in the cold nights.
My friends are
my horse,
my wolf,
and my falcon.

I bathe as usual
by the waterfall
near my cabin.
All of a sudden
a bright light shines on me.
I turn and see that the water that I'm bathing in
flows directly from ABBA's sacred fountain.
The water is pure.
It rejuvenates me.
It cools me.
It heals me.

A SAD NOVEMBER

My cousin dies of cancer.
In the hospital my uncle's wife is killed.
Madrina is like an oak, but not recognizing anyone
reached
the day written in the Sacred Book.

Facing so many deaths at once I went to Freeport.
My partner – The Bible.
My compact discs contained
meditations and lessons on
the Word of God.

I rest.
I wait to hear Abba's voice
as I've heard It so many other times.
I did not hear Him. I saw Him.
I went out to the balcony and He was there.
In front of me the sea.
To my left the sun was coming out.
Venus, the planet of love, was in the middle.
To my right, the moon was saying goodbye.

Message—
Nothing dies.
All is transformed by the Love of God.

ROSES BY THE SEA
6/1/11

Beautiful pink roses,
you who are perfect life
from the moment you bloom
you remind me
of God's perfect plan for me.

Beautiful pink roses,
as delicate as you may seem against
the ominous sea,
you remind me that no matter how big a problem I may face,
God's perfect love will save me.

THE GARDEN
6/2/11

Only green…
Not much of a variety of colors.
Only peace and silence…

A bench perfect for two…
I seat.
Christ and I,
friends for life.
Sharing, laughing…
Knowing we are ONE.

THE RED CHAIR

6/1/11

Red is love.
Red is passion.
Red is blood.
Here I am today seating with you.
The birds sing.
My feet touch the coolness of the earth.
I feel Pachamama's vibration and love
through my feet
lulling me to sleep.

As I surrender to that sleep
I reach out to the infinite
and I become one with the warmth of the sun.

The breeze caresses me
To make sure all is pleasing to me.

The birds continue their symphony of joy.
And only the blue sky
is
the witness of God's perfect balance in my life.
Love. Passion. Life.

THE BRIDGE
6/2/11

We are all in a journey from birth to death.
We all cross a physical bridge
at some time in our lives.
We leave something or someone behind
and
cross over to something new, exiting and mysterious.

We all cross the spiritual bridge
every day in our lives.
Night into day;
day into night.

How great it is
to wake up excited
to live the new day with all its mysteries
and
possibilities.

Move from day into night.
Never to die.

MOTHER AND CHILD

6/2011

Mother,
when I look at you, I feel peace.
I feel respect for the pain you endured
when you lost your Son.
Tenderness seeing how you carry
your Son in your arms.
Physical and spiritual strength
for having resisted with fortitude
the vexations done to your Son.

Mother, you are my compass.
With you as my north
I will fulfill
my Sacred Covenant.

A BABY'S PERFECTION

In a baby's eyes: the sky.
In the smile: jingle bells.

In the skin: the temple of the Holy Spirit
In the hands: creation.
In the feet: evolution.

INFINITE WISDOM

Infinite Wisdom
Infinite Light
Blessed be Your name.

Praise to You, Father,
for all the love you've brought to my life.

May the person you have chosen for me and I always
walk in Your love and do Your will.

FORGIVE ME LORD

My Lord, forgive me if I cry.
It is not that I am ungrateful;
it is just that I am sad
thinking that my heart will be torn
the day he leaves.

I only have the joy of knowing
that
I will be able to say,

"Thank you for the warmth of his body.
It is more powerful
than the sun,
hotter than a bonfire.

Thank you for giving me
his aquamarine eyes
because for the first time
in their reflection
I saw myself as a woman.

Thank you for his white silky hands
that tenderly
caressed my body inviting me to be his.

Thank you for his strong arms
where so many times I surrender in a frenzied rapture.

Thank you for his pure spirit
because he nurtured me
so I would not perish."

A PRAYER OF THANKSGIVING[2]

Thank you Father
for the sun and the moon
for they remind me
of your ever present love and guidance.

Thank you for the brightest star
for it reminds me of Jesus
becoming flesh and dwelling
among us to bring salvation
and freedom from sin.

Thank you for the waters
of the rivers and the sea
for they washed away original sin
in baptism.

Thank you for the wind
the Breath of Life—
the Holy Spirit
through whose guidance
we ward evil and temptation.

Thank you for the birds' song
for they are the choir
of angel and saints
the bells that toll
for happiness and the constant chant—
PRAISE THE LORD ALL MY SOUL!
PRAISE HIS HOLY NAME!

HELP ME LORD

Lord, You who saw my birth;
You who created me;
light my way
so that I may see your power.

Divine Power
I will not fear you.
Let me know Your mysteries
so that I can take you by the hand
to others that have need of You.

If you find me unworthy, Lord,
remember that I am human
and at times my spirit is weak
and I am dragged by currents of emotions
that are unclean before Your eyes.

Lord, deign to see my sacrifice
and my desire to be better
so you give me access
to scale the mountain
so one day I can arrive to You
Pure!

GOLD AND PEARL

Thank you, Lord
for this great day of a spectacular
sunrise and a dazzling sunset.

The hues of the colors at dusk were vibrating playfully
awakening our senses gradually
until the sunset wrapped all things
in a loving,
lulling penumbra
of infinite sensibility,
opening the way for the queen of the night.

She appeared dressed in a soft orange
and as she ascended the steps to her throne
she started to turn into a brilliant
white.
She arrived at the top and remained there
dazzling the people that were admiring her beauty.
The background was a tapestry of black velvet
with inlay of gold and silver;
of glass and stalactite.

The spectacular show ends
and she descends slowly the steps
radiating her majestic presence
disappearing through the western door
to appear magnanimous over
the grey-like pyramids of Egypt.

LOVE,

A

MASTERPIECE

AT

WORK

MARRIAGE

Brutality

Oppression

Deterioration

Set back

Illiteracy

Repeal

Contempt

Insecurity

Dissonance

DIVORCE

Sweetness

Liberty

Courage

Progress

Culture

Flatter

Appreciation

Being

Assonance

THE GLORY!

Joyful twenty-three…
Five of understanding …
Loving twenty-three…
One of luck…
Twenty-three of sensible reality…
Five powerful leader…
Twenty-three-Marvelous!

THE ANGLO-SAXON QUIJOTE

I was looking at Don Quijote

and I thought I was dreaming

I do not know what nonsense…

My God!

It is not Don Quijote! No!

It is he!

The one that transformed me from Aldonza to Dulcinea.

I'm no longer the cleaning woman of a muleteer

I am now a pampered princess

with the freedom to ask

and seeing it granted.

Sweet Don Quijote,

thank you for awakening

the soul of a young girl

into

the soul of a woman;

the soul of a mother;

the soul of a dove;

the soul of a lioness;

the sublime soul

of

creativity and pleasure.

PALOMINO[3]

Beautiful palomino golden like the wheat.
Body perfectly lean,
esthetically contoured
to the savagery of the plains
to the body of the mares in need of his love.

The mountains in the background
are emeralds and dark ruby.
The sky rose pink and black purple.
Trees reaching for God
in the everlasting communion
of relative poles –
calm and storm;
dryness and inundation;
fertility and barren soil;
home of the homeless.

As you stand there my Palomino
your mane floats in the wind
and I'm reminded
of the beauty of freedom;
of the strength I feel
as I watch you being ever so close to me,
knowing you are forever mine.

WHO IS THIS MAN?

9/5/93

Who is this man
that offers me a clean sugar cane
so I may chew the bagasse
and enjoy the sweet juice;

that offers me that red pomegranate
so that I may squeeze it
and extract each seed
augmenting my pleasure with each one;

that offers me an opened
coconut,
so that the pure water
it holds refreshes me;

and offers me the vine
like a pavilion
so I may sleep in his lap?

THE ENCHANTED SAXOPHONE

[Inspiration -- *Europa* – Musical Composition
Interpreted
by Gato Barbieri]

The seductive music kisses my body.
The saxophone speaks sweetly to me,
soflty breathing in my ears.
Its rhythm increases and is as though
we were playing and laughing;
swiftly changing to a slow pace.
Its hands move slowly
on my body.
It arrives at the lower part of my back
and gently squeezes me.
The music is now like a strong wave,
like the swaying of the tree
moved by the breeze.
I fly!
I can't think straight.
I transport myself to who knows where,
but everything is beautiful and finally I understand
the meaning of: PERFECTION.

I KNOW

I know that you were for me
wealth of pleasure and of sadness;
essential equilibrium for a good love novel.
All is boring and lethargic without you.
Without you I do not begin in *do* but in *si.*

For you and only for you I surrendered without reservation,
never thinking of tomorrow.
The promise was in the present not in the future.
Each day became an immediate past.

What can I do now that I do not have you?
What can I do?
I have nothing.
Bare your soul to me without fear.
You will see that you need me now as much as you did yesterday.

Come without thinking who I was.
Come because I want to be something better.
I want to be intimately wrapped in your body
like the ivy, adhering firmly to your inner most being.

A SEDUCTIVE AFTERNOON
7/2011

Golden fields of Castille…

Warm *siestas…*

Limitless fields…

Multicolored rosebushes surround my house.

It is dusk.

My lover is seated on a blue chair.

By the cool shade of the white house

he plays the guitar.

I, in my kitchen, prepare

a succulent dish for my man.

Like a serpent

the music enters through the window.

It captures me.

I have to stop.

The rhythm of the music and the *cante jondo* of my lover

begin to burn my blood.

I can't resist it.

I turn the stove off.

Subtly I approach my lover.
I caress him.
I gently bite his earlobe.
I run my hands by his chest.
My *duende* is awakened by
the smell of earth and sun that his body exudes.

My lover knows what I want.
My lover takes me in his arms
and plays with my body with the same
intensity he had played the guitar with.
His dexterity makes me experience
the little death
so that I may wake up
to the infinite love of the universe.

THINKING OF HIM[4]
(Meditations)

When I think of him
> my body exudes
> the exquisite fragrance
> of the sweetest aroma
> of a gardenia.

I think of

> the exquisite and rich honey
> of the beehive of the forest;
> of a quiet and warmth brook
> passing lightly over my body;
> of the bright colors of the prism
> bursting like a volcano.

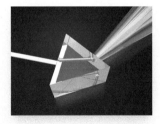

When I think of him
> I drink the fresh and delicious sap
> of the desert cactus.

MY MAJO

His black hair
like the night
with
starry reflections
tempts me.

His body
like
the mustard tree
is strong

His shoulders
are
wide and robust.

His chest
perfect for me to recline my head on it
and feel the beats
of his heart.

His arms
like branches
stretch out offering
shelter and protection.

His legs
are
the promise of long walks
by
paths lit by the sun.

And his laughter?
IS
an earthquake
that shakes my body
and awakens the tigress in me,
my bacanal side.

DIURNAL SOLITUDE
10/16/85

My sky sadly cries
for the loss of the red rose,
the lilac chrysanthemum
and for the breeze that flows from the river or the sea.

Tender moments…
unmistakable smell of the faithful partner…
deep breath…
funny snoring sounds that embarrasses him upon awakening…

Diurnal solitude…
unending cycle…
uncertain future…

YOU ARE TO MY SENSES...

10/26/86

You are sweet and juicy
like a pulpy mamey;
a succulent guava;

an exhilarating and
      melting chocolate
in my mouth;

a fresh breeze;
the scent of the rose and the pine;

a magnificent marble that takes shape
at the command of my hand;
Bethoven's Apasionata
        or
Chopin's Nocturne;
        you are
in all my surroundings—the sky, the sun, the nights.

BOHEMIAN NIGHT

12/23/86

Bohemian night…
Souls that at night
search to satiate their thirst for fantasy.
All brothers, united
by the umbilical cord
of melancholy, love and pure rhythm.

Glorious moment!

Bobby sings
and I am absorbed by the mural
and I find myself hugging Morito
full of joy;
and from there
to become an ethereal dancer
and in a flash
I am a guitar player in a café.
In the penumbra
I play *boleros, rumbas* and everything
else that pleases my nocturnal brothers.

THINKING OF YOU
(Meditaciones)[5]

You are my tasteful and forbidden fruit,
my liberator and my conquistador,
meaningful truth and barrier of hope,
my beacon and my darkness.

Alone, my thoughts are like sand
scattered but still.
Trembling and burning underneath you,
my sun.
Cooled by your eyes,
my skies.
Engulfed by the slashing and thrust
of your body, my sea.

--Oh, misery! Night is here.
So is the tide.
How is it that you are back so soon?
Why do you bring with you
so many tormenting thoughts?
They tear my soul to pieces!
Why won't you let me enjoy
the peacefulness and calmness
of the day?
Why won't you?

Is there real peace during the day?
I lethargically look up to the skies
and see the white clouds,
the messengers of the One Truth:
To live is to see what we have seen return.
It is seeing everything again--anguish,
happiness, hopes[6] and dreams.

---

[5] Copyright. July 18, 1988. Registration Number 331-197

[6] "Las nubes" de Azorín. Marín, Diego, Literatura Española. New York: Holt, Rinehart and Winston, 1968.

Like the clouds you are there
with each passing day,
only to fade away into a darkness
that hunts and gnaws my soul.

You'll come and you'll go.
That's life!
When there is honey
I'll suck it in delight.
When there is pain
I'll lull it
with the memories of laughter and pleasure.

FLEETING THOUGHT
7/29/85

Dessert of strawberries with cream
fragrance of brandy
fiery blaze.

SONG OF JOY

1985

You are so far away!
And then,
you are so close!

You are far
when I think
I cannot touch you,
I cannot kiss you,
I cannot adore you,
I cannot be one with you.

But there is no distance
when I daydream and I:
touch you,
I kiss you,
I adore you,
I caress you until I am one with you.

I am reborn.
I live again.
I dream again.
I am.

THE SUMMER HOME[7]

Warm, summer breeze!
Treble of light!
Morning of glory!

Sumptuous sounds of a roaring sea
bathing
the clean sands of the universe.

Crystal waters that sooth my soul
as I stand in the porch with
my wife.
She is dressed in a white dress
sensuously caressing the flesh
to match the beauty
of a virginal maiden.

I'm also dressed in white to feel
ethereal;
one with all that surrounds me.

Around us the barren land is
decorated
with sparkling green grass
that sways to the compass of the
playful wind.

Lethargic afternoons
of endless conversations
in a home
that's miles away from the rest
of mankind,
yet as close as our
hearth is to our chimney.

---

[7]   Copyright. Registration Number 331-196. July 18.1988

Autumnal sunset that promises
the eternal flux
of life everlasting;
of the concurrent seasons
of limitless space.

FREE SLAVE

Today, more than ever I yearn
for the love of a man
that does not say;
"You are mine."
But;
"I feel good by your side."
A man that does not judge the silence of a night
as a failure,
but
as a time of introspection,
of growth, of bonding.

I yearn for a man
that makes me his slave
letting me BE.

EACH DAY A CANVAS

SPANISH IMPROVISATIONS

Brook
Stream that wind through the world
of undaunted mountains,
wash my feet and my soul,
wash me
that I may become sweeter,
so that love may come to me.

"Amapolas"
When I die…
cover my grave with poppies
so the red
reminds my friends of
my love
FOR LIFE
AND MY PASSION.

"Cancioncilla"
I want you. I want you.
I want you just for me.

I want you.
I want you like no other I've ever wanted.

I want you. I want you.
I want you just for me.

I want you **chulapo,**
unpredictable and full of life.

EACH DAY A CANVAS

Life is a wonderful collection of art.
We move through the gallery of time
and make an impression in each space.

Our fears, worry, pain and hopelessness
create bizarre and grotesque paintings.

Great is the moment when we can superimpose on the former
a prism of bright colors
which burst forth from our happiness and peaceful moments.

Every second is precious.
Live the moment.
Savor the sun, rain, air, and the earth.

EGYPT
LAND OF CONTRAST
7/2011

Sultans with oil wells.
Farmers cultivating their fields.

Powerful men
go to work in big air condition cars.
The meek man
On his donkey
travels underneath
a scorching sun
that reverberates and
consumes
all that is not shielded from its rays.

Small town
in the middle of the desert
barely alive.

The Valley of the Kings
close by
filled with splendor
and
a rich history
of a past that will never ever return.

The Nile River and the desert are
inseparable friends.
At the bank of the Nile
makeshift homes.
In the desert castles
that have lasted centuries
and
pyramids that preserve the secret
of a great civilization that will never return.

PLAZA MAYOR OF SALAMANCA

7/2011

You are the great historical hotel.
Your walls have
medallions of historical figures
that have changed men's destiny.

Your center is the great lobby
that welcomes foreigners
from all parts of the world.

The benches in the center
invites us to sit on them
and as a family celebrate
weddings,
baptisms,
birthdays
and
more.

Through your lobby the regulars
stroll
and visit you every day
to
share with their friends
the day's occurrence
in the language of Cervantes.

Your clock
not only gives the time
but
it is also the
key point
where friends and lovers find each other.

Your balconies embroider
your walls in black thread
with golden beads
that reflect the sun
that shines on you
on
the four cardinal points.

How many times have I sat here, with you,
enjoying life!

Here I find my tranquility.
I breathe peace in the midst
of the multitude that like the waves of the sea
crash on the shore without ceasing.
Here I laugh and sing with the Tuna
in the warm and cold nights

Here I saw Spain
win the UEFA 2008.
I was dining in the plaza
enjoying the celebration around me when I saw
a small dog, that like me
was a silent observer.
We were living the moment.
He and I were observing
the fans' enthusiasm,
and the generations of parents, children and grandparents pass.

The bells of your tower toll
and remind me of the passing of time.
I fall in a trance and hypnotized
I travel back to Sancti-Spíritu
where I lived a safe, secure and joyful youth
without ever thinking
that one day
I would be here,
in your lobby
in the very heart of your city.

QUIETUDE

12/8/1971

The conductor turns.
Pulls his dress coat
and raises his hands and leaves them up
for a few seconds.
The bright lights
dim slowly
while at the same time
the sullen notes of the
Pathétique de Tchaickowsky
unfold.

Nikolay Denisov © 123RF.COM

SAILBOAT IN THE NILE
7/2011

The sun sets slowly.
The sailor sails parallel to the light
to enjoy the spectrum of the colors created
by
THE GREAT MASTER

LIFE AND DEATH

Our selfishness can only bring darkness and slavery
of mind and body.
Sometimes we love so much
that we cannot let go.
But it is easy to let go if we
only look at the promise of light and life
given by the sun and the moon.

Were the sun to shine constantly its force
would be destructive.
Trees would burn,
the earth would be dry
and
human beings would dehydrate.

Darkness must come
to bring harmony and balance.

The warm and golden colors
of the sunset precede darkness
to remind us that we have lived another day
in all its fullness.

Soon the moon rises
and with it we are reminded
that the light of a new day
is forever present.

LIGHT IS:

forever constant in the universe;

it is energy;

it is The Truth.

The sun and the moon

are reminders

that darkness is but a momentary lapse

or transition, NOT THE END.

VISUALIZATION AND IMAGINATION

In <u>Creating Health</u> by Deepak Chopra, M.D. he states, "When nature is unbalanced, the whole is endangered by disruptions in its parts. To be healthy, all natural beings must interact with nature through open and balanced channels of intelligence. The value of change, or dynamism, must be balanced with nonchange, or stability. Our word for this is *homeostasis*— the balance of functions that keeps a living organism's physiology in equilibrium."[8]

I invite you to imagine and visualize yourself as one with all that is good and perfect – Nature. It is perfect because whether I see it as Abba's Creation where I have always found joy, comfort and peace; you will have the same experiences even though you see it as the creation of the god of your forefathers. Live each day as though it was your last. Thank your Creator for giving you life, your partner (husband or wife) a friend, your children, your pet, your colleague(s) at work and on and on. Live giving thanks. Edify another whenever you get a chance to do so. Remember, "The Word was the source of life, and this life brought light to mankind. The light shines in the darkness, and the darkness has never put it out."[9]

May the life and light you give to others be returned to you so that, "Your strength be renewed. You rise on wings like eagles; run and not get weary; walk and not grow weak."[10]

---

[8]   Deepak Chopra. *Creating Health. How to Wake Up the Body's Intelligence.* Revised Edition. (New York: Houghton Mifflin Company, 1987)

[9]   *Good News Bible with Deuterocanocicals/Apocrypha.* John 1:4-5. (New York: American Bible Society, 1976)

[10]   Ibid. Isaiah 40:31

CREDIT FOR EDITORIAL USAGE

Printed in the United States
By Bookmasters